Robert Walser
Thirty Poems

Robert Walser
Thirty Poems

Selected and translated
by Christopher Middleton

Christine Burgin / New Directions
New York

Acknowledgments for twelve of the microscript translations and for "Rilke," "To Georg
Trakl," "Pascin," and "Sentiment" to *PN Review* (Carcanet Press, Manchester, U.K.);
and for "The Furnished Room," "Apparently you're very poor," and "Lindbergh" to
The Swiss Institute, New York, publishers of *Fragments of Imaginary Landscapes*, 1994.

Cover drawing by Karl Walser reproduced courtesy Musée Neuhaus Bienne,
Depositum Fondation/Stiftung Gottfried Keller © GKS, Zürich, 2011
Walser manuscripts pages 12, 26, and 50:
copyright © the Robert Walser Foundation, Bern, Switzerland

Robert Walser: Thirty Poems is a co-publication by
New Directions Publishing and the Christine Burgin Gallery.

Manufactured in the United States of America
New Directions Books are printed on acid-free paper.
First published as a New Directions/Christine Burgin hardbound book in 2012

Design and composition by Laura Lindgren

Library of Congress Cataloging-in-Publication Data
Walser, Robert, 1878–1956.
  Thirty poems / Robert Walser ; selected and translated
by Christopher Middleton.
     p.   cm.
  ISBN 978-0-8112-2001-9 (alk. paper)
  I. Middleton, Christopher, 1926–. II. Title.
  PT2647.A64T45 2012
  831'.912–dc23 2011048682

New Directions Books are published for James Laughlin by
New Directions Publishing Corporation
80 Eighth Avenue, New York, New York 10011

Christine Burgin books are published by
The Christine Burgin Gallery
239 West 18th Street, New York, New York 10011

Contents

From the Microscripts

Now known chiefly as a writer of eccentric and exquisitely playful prose, Robert Walser (1878–1956) was essentially a poet, and editors now place his poems in two main groups. I have used *Gedichte und Dramolette*, vol. 11 of *Das Gesamtwerk*, 1971 (vol. 13 in the later *Samtliche Werke*, 1978–85) and *Aus dem Bleistiftgebiet*, vol. 6, 2000, the province of Walser's microscripts.

Filling more than five hundred pages, the poems face a translator with quite a wild prospect. Besides, Walser's first collection, *Gedichte* (1909, reprinted without change or addition in 1918), is so deeply sequestered in German *Lied* conventions — of wispy singable delicacies — that today's translator has, or so I decided, to derive his versions almost exclusively from work of the 1920s. Walser published precious little after 1932; the only hiatus in his earlier years occurred before, during, and after the First World War.

Another limitation comes with Walser's tendency to rhyme profusely. A large number of his poems are, as regards prosody, singularly conventional, if not jejune: the jingle of rhyme lowers the true voice of feeling.

To enlarge on this limitation somewhat: Walser loved to rhyme and had a great facility for it. In some poems of four- or five-stress lines, he'll even allow a rhyme — the first that came into his head — to direct the poem's development, to dictate what comes next. But the potential for *errance*, spontaneity, improvisation, is throttled by the insipidity of many rhymes, by their perfunctory character. The rhymes are so used up that, like antique doorsteps, they are worn down.

To translate poems with such rhyme schemes would call for a virtuoso like Byron or Auden to reinvent the German (as Rosmarie Waldrop has done with her versions of Oskar Pastior). However, the challenge would not be accepted, because the poems, for all their jejune charms, are trite. I have even found one poem, "Der Rabe" (1928–29), in which, out of twenty-eight lines, twenty-one reiterate the vowel *a*, long or short, in mimicry of a raven's call. Even Li Po, let us not forget, had sometimes to turn out consumer poems; Walser may have hoped that his lyrics might even be rewarded by readers of feuilletons.

My selection is limited to the 1920s, the decade after Walser's apparent First World War hiatus. Some of the rhymed poems of that period I could "tweak," but only one poem (unrhymed) is a paraphrase: translating calls for respect for the ins and outs of the original. Yet some translations had to rhyme intermittently where the original rhymed continuously. Among the microscripts are also poems that rhyme only in the last two lines. Not to be mimed or even echoed were Walser's Swiss-German intonational patterns.

When it is called for, I add, after a translation, details of the original's provenance, once or twice a reminder of its prosody. *G* stands for *Gedichte*, *M* for microscripts.

For various reasons the two sources are kept separate. *Gedichte* poems of the 1920s are the texts that Walser did finish, submitting many to periodicals and newspapers, as indicated at the foot of a translation. The *Bleistiftgebiet* writings, deciphered over a period of twenty years by Werner Morlang and Bernhard Echte, and now filling six volumes, may not have been finished to Walser's satisfaction. With a fine miniature calligraphic hand he penciled all his inventions on hundreds of scraps of waste paper — old bills, the backs of telegrams, rejection or acceptance slips. Though some texts did appear in a finished form (a fact that initiated their being deciphered), most constituted a huge store of materials on which Walser could have drawn, should (as he feared) his earning power have dwindled, and if he had not been in June 1933 transferred to the Herisau insane asylum.

Harlequin though he was, Walser took pride in being a "son of the working people." Self-educated, he stands apart from the intellectual rulers of twentieth-century poetry, but his poems are not all idyllic. They spring immediately from a binary opposition between idyll and its ruin, such opposition being a perennial source of poetic art, imaginative play, and revolt.

This translator hopes that his selection shows Walser's poetry at its closest to his vistas across experience; at the same time, I would not swear that his microcosm is to be rediscovered as a system of avant-garde thrusts. But I do draw attention to a (perhaps anomalous) poem, "The Young Man in the Carpathians." The wording as such almost hushes up the gist; convex wording is shadowed by a concave implication—that the young man's innocence prevents him from seeing that he is cannon fodder. Harmless as the wording may be felt to be, it signals the diabolic ghastliness with which the First World War shook Walser's microcosm apart.

Christopher Middleton

From *Gedichte und Dramolette*

Weiße Büsche.

Die weiße Büsche regt sich leis
im Garten, und im rauhen Wind,
der wunderlich vom Himmel kommt.
Der Himmel ist halb still, halb wild;
halb läßt er sich in Wolken gehn,
halb tritt er Theil hervor im Blau.
Die Sonne ist vergessen schon
und es bereitet sich die Welt

in einen Garten einzugehn,
den Abend; weiße Büsche regt
im Abend und im rauhen Wind
im Abendwind, regt in mir auch
etwas wie lustige Büsche sich?
Ich glaub es nicht, die weiße Nacht
ist hier schon gänzlich Herrscherin.
In mir regt sich kein Lüstchen mehr.

White Linen

A little movement stirs the linen,
it's in the garden, in the wind
which comes, a marvel, from the sky.
The sky is halfway still, half wild;
half it is involved with cloud,
half stepping brightly out in blue.
Already the sun has been forgotten
and all the world is making ready
to disappear into a garden
which is evening; white the linen
stirs in a gentle wind, the evening
wind, does it make a sort of linen
airily also stir in me?
I don't believe so. Quiet night
has just become entirely sovereign.
The breeze in me now stirs no more.

c. 1901. Translated from a facsimile of the manuscript (illustrated opposite),
as reproduced in Robert Walser, *Saite und Sehnsucht*, edited by Elio Fröhlich
(Berlin: Suhrkamp Verlag, 1979).

Chopin

How nice it is, you listen to him,
all at once he makes you dream
and fantasize. If till today
you never loved, now you become
a lover and belong no more
only to yourself, and so are glad.
O the bliss, to think no longer
of your own poor self, to feel
rich since now all feeling is
free from a common self's restraint.
Chopin's sounds, are they curls,
seductive smiles, the aroma
of Egyptian cigarettes,
the shapes and fragrances of flowers?
How the heart blossoms now, and soul
is reveling in its own delight.
A marvelous and golden chasm
opens to you, evening sun
caresses you, in another
country where the goings-on
are softer far and far more tender,
quieter and more fancy-free,
tall trees shade you, bright and dark

blend in delicious melodies,
where sorrow's beautiful, despondency
glorious, just like his music,
his, the Pole who, years ago,
performed at concert halls in Paris,
played for all, soldiers, simple
working people, bankers, ministers.
By the dalliance of his hands
who was not snatched up in amazement?
Audiences were charmed, the scoffer
Heinrich Heine loved and honored him.
He played as if he did so wholly
by himself, society
and solitude were to him the same,
yet in the tumult of the world
he gave perhaps his uttermost,
and his playing was so beautiful
because it pleased him to be granted
the right to do so. Sensibility,
if noble, has the need to give.

G 162–63. Published September 1920 in *Die Weltbuhne*.
Unrhymed iambic tetrameters.

The Creature

There is a rustling of animals at night,
they breathe like us.
Have you ever felt it,
this Substance with a thousand wounds
at moments when it's quiet in the mountains,
up in the cold air,
in this Nature, this Crypt?—
Do not be cross with me,
even if from a hundred mouths
it had in you disparaged me,
still I honor you!
Everybody quarrels with himself,
climbs from the summit of his discontent
slowly into the vale
on paths as small
as tongues pronouncing attitudes
which have swung around,
and everybody reverts, deserting spirit,
into a bit of happiness,
to take a distance from what they imagined.
Have you seen it, with great eyes
standing in the forest, the creature
that witnessed wars against the Huns?

Last night I did come close to her.
Now here I sit.
The locomotives race across the lands.
Across the ocean fly the ships.

G 396–97. Published in *Prager Tagblatt*, October 1925.

Daniel in the Lions' Den

Perhaps their stomachs at the time were full
and to assault their prey did not occur to them.
O he gave them such a terrifying look that, scared,
to them it seemed to stream straight out of him
like a flower of flame. On the edge of the den
aromas then arose, a jubilation, clamor, like
a divine criminal's victory it smelled to them.
The fragrance reached the nose of those
who'd wanted only his downfall, but now
they had to watch with great astonishment
how the kindly lamp of life in him
made his shaggy judges shy away.
What was it then the lions could smell?
The small body and great soul of Daniel?

G. 280. Written 1925. Published in *Prager Presse*, October 1927.
Rhymed pentameter couplets.

The Crucified

Here the whip and rod are hanging
that for all the love and goodness
he had given, they gave him
that he might revel in his torment.
His punishment was all the harsher
since piety made him a sheep.
O my little Jesus child,
alas, you did not keep your glow,
and for no other reason you
went pitifully to the dogs.
The brutal hand that wounds you still
at any time is a big mouth.
Now and then you should have read, full
of fun, at least a penny dreadful
and smiled as well at all the people.
In general, what once was swaddled
comes to be riffraff, rude and addled.
If only your culture and good taste
had landed you with a fan on cushions,
not thrashed and lashed and flayed
as in museums you're portrayed.

G 286. Published in *Prager Tagblatt*, December 1926.
Rhymed tetrameter couplets.

Rilke

In a lonely château
not long ago
somewhat of an exile
on the horse anent Pegasus
you rode, rather serious,
with seldom a smile
in landscapes of mood
that flashed and glowed
you strove for the truth
of importunate Youth.
Hard for the Poem you fought.
Now be at peace, adorn,
shimmering fruit
in a shapely bowl,
the lyric pavilion.
Unruffled repose,
when duty is done
and off you shake,
each by each,
life's traveling shoes,
is beauty enough.
I was content to make
beside your grave
this little speech.

G 330. Published in *Prager Presse*, January 4, 1927.

Marginal Note

It was at a gala party that a celebrated gent
said that it was plain to him that pleasure was my bent.

If in the future someone's giving me the push,
I'll tell him international understanding calls for him to hush.

Anyone who went to a school Napoleon chose to found
could never think he'd come to have a disunited mind.

A splendid building can be mirrored in a puddle any day.
Once I doffed my cap in passing, now respect has drained away.

It's at the desk you leave your cash to hear a poet thunder.
Into his hat you drop a coin to please the organ-grinder.

Contentedly I watched as over collars flatirons steamed,
it took me back to when, right there, the City Council had
                                                    convened.

Deep into fundamentals, is there anywhere to go?
I know the score, a sideliner perhaps, but it is better so.

C 359–60. Published in *Neue Schweizer Rundschau*, July 1927.

Lindbergh

(a paraphrase)

O how they pique me, the chestnut flambeaux
in gardens of the municipal offices! So
should I start
on a long country walk? Would it pay?
Must a man always be seeking experience,
writing about it?

                    Only the other day,
a mother I chaffed talked and talked to me,
straight from the heart,
of troubles that vexed her:
me being the next
best thing to a "figure," bundles of
free magazines, bigger and bigger
anyway thump my door.

                    It's nice, to be sure,
when a chambermaid shines your shoes, but,
sakes alive, this
North American boy, who's
done such a spirited deed at age twenty-five,
makes me, more so than ever, exacting:

Rave as folks may about his panache,
it's not my style to prattle and gush
or descant on "art" and that kind of thing.

G 293. 1927.

Sentiment

Whatever it was in plain sight
gave me fresh heart, if, nonetheless
it could not, being nature, give me rest,
soon it will be far away, outside.

I'll go without it then, this glow,
this ringing of the sounds and of the colors,
and with a passion sing of it. Somehow, as if
what's missing left me with a mystery,
its absence makes me love it all twice over.

Once you have seen it with your inward eye,
a beautiful thing spreads beauty all around.
To dote on it, or want it back again, is wrong.
It walks along with you, kept well in mind.

G 244. October 1927.

The Newspaper

Pondering coolly in my thoughts
my future and my losses,
I peered down from the point I stood on
across unruffled lake waters
where swans moved like women,
as if they performed a ceremony.
Prettily painted boats came and went
to and fro, and the mountain
swam in the mirror
just as aptly as a person of spirit
delights in life and in the charm
of a fine sorrow the soul shudders. Later,
while the whisper of branches
made itself audible from trees
and I was walking down the hill,
I spread out the newspaper.

G 403. 1930. Unrhymed loosely alternating pentameters and hexameters.

Der Jüngling in den Karpathen

Von Robert Walser.

An seine Freundin denkend,
die in der Stube zu ebener Erde
wirtschaftete, lag der Jüngling,
den geschmeidigen Körper
im Grase hingelegt. Auf der Straße,
die das Gebirge durchschnitt,
marschierten Regimenter.
Aus bläulichumflorter
Ferne klang die Musik
der Schlacht, es hörte sich
wie ein Traum an. Dreien Mädchen,
auf den Hügel spazierend,
entfloh ein Lied, und die blühenden
Wiesen und der Wald
schienen miteinzustimmen.
Ein alter Mann begleitete
die Sängerinnen, vor denen,
als sie ausgesungen hatten, der Jüngling
seinen Hut aus Achtung vor dem Süßen
und Tröstenden abzog,
das für ihn von den schicksalverherrlichenden
Lippen geklungen.

The Young Man in the Carpathians

Thinking about his best girl
busy with the housework
in the downstairs room,
the young man lay, supple in body,
stretched out in the grass.
On the road that cut through the mountains
regiments were marching.
Battle music sounded
from the blue enveloping the distance,
heard as in a dream. Three girls
were walking on the hill, from them
a song escaped, and flowers,
meadows, and the woodland,
seemed to be joining in.
An old man walked along
accompanying the singing;
out of respect for the sweet
consoling thing
that had sounded for him
from lips glorifying fate,
the young man doffed his hat.

G 242. Published in *Prager Presse*, December 1927 (illustrated opposite).
Free verse.

To Georg Trakl

In a foreign country I might be reading you
or just as well at home
and your verses were a pleasure to me always;
definitely in the room,
round me the radiance, the shimmer
of marvelous expressions you had found,
never once was any thought of mine forlorn.
A clinging mantle seemed to clothe me
there, in the abyss of reading,
intent upon the beauty of your being,
which is the swan, the boat, the garden
and the atmospheres they too dispense
as up they float, you, opulent
with leaves, ineffable soul, lissom oak,
tumbled rock, whisk of a mouse's tail,
a little girl, her dancing, yours, dejected giant,
here on a meadow in the Jura where
in play, as if I dreamed it, I propose
this address to your genius.
Did some perpetuation of the fate
of Hölderlin reverberate around your cradle
and keeping you company, as life went on,
doom you at last to golden lunacy?

Your poems, when I read them, more and more
carry me away as in a splendid coach and four.

G 336. February 1928.

The Furnished Room

Put too much in your place,
you only shrink the space.
Pictures, furniture in excess
can make a room a dreadful mess.
Wardrobe, bed, chair, and couch
deprave its trimness with debauch.
Several other things as well
in the room are laughable.
Conches, figurines, and vases
have woozy, wheezy, whispering voices.
Pillows, blankets, shaggy mats,
ill-assorted, do not match
the notion of a now and here.
Vanished times in knickknacks bare
teeth too sensitive, gnaw away
the fabric special to each day.
A room is brighter and more spacious,
cleverer and more bodacious,
if you forbear to place
over its primal face —
by stuffing every crack with ornament —
another that's more lush, more opulent.
The room itself will then bestow
upon the room a quality, a glow.

Too much knowledge, multitudes of skill
some folks could jettison, they might as well.
One would be more
without humungous stuff inside one's door.
Not letting go ages and freezes you,
perpetual retention causes wrinkles too.
A room was never meant to bode the worst,
so let it stay the way you saw it first.

G 274. Written 1928–29. Published in *Prager Presse*, June 1932.

Pascin

A little prudish, a little crude
his drawings are mostly of comical things,
I mean that the line his pencil has spent
is dainty, but also impudent.
I owned a picture of his: the maid
told me to hide it from her sight.
On Potsdamerstrasse, in the glow
from a musical cabaret's window,
our two persons met one night.
We talked in whispers for a while.
As I walked home, I saw a crew
of workmen still with work to do.
Sometimes his pictures,
combining nasty things with nice,
have attracted critics' strictures.
Divinely Lukas Cranach could
portray his nudities naïve
and naturally dignified.
You certainly will run a risk
when daintiness makes you a prude;
so we walk on and our hurts frisk
like puppydoggies at our side.

G 291. July 1930. [Jules Pascin, painter and graphic artist]

Kennst du Sie?

She who wears the long gloves,
have you seen her ever?
The passion you began with,
all at once it's over.

Spread in time around you
a prospect full of laughter;
taking fright it disappeared.
Has she never found you?

She took a mood quite early
to make on me her mark;
everywhere was clarity
till she left me in the dark.

The lady, whom one does not love,
as long as there were people
who swung up to a height,
she never leaves them quite.

G 402. 1930.

From the Microscripts

A woman's awe-inspiring blouse

A woman's awe-inspiring blouse
is hanging on a wall inside a house.
What splendid lines to start some poetry.
Might any other thoughts occur to me?
On the porch that I am looking over
(with eyes in which one should be a believer,
while busily building up on what they scan)
sits a skyblue painted water can—
behind an opulent umbrella, fruit
of an established firm of old repute—
in an invisible bathtub, what is more,
a girl, at this beguiling early hour,
tones up her measured rounds with nothing wetter
than fondling wet, a table next, a letter,
a tiny little letter on it, trifles
away, encircled sweetly by its riffles
and decorative garlands, thus, the time
I shorten with a pleasure quite sublime
by turning versicles that chance to rhyme.
Astonishingly prosaic they may sound, but I'm
unaware of any obligation else.
Can that be pickled fish this poet smells?
It conjures up a hungriness in me.

Meanwhile I find it unbelievably
beautiful how softly now the thin
branches move to whispers of the wind's violin,
and falling also silent, now I will
lean, rapturous, across the windowsill.

M 513b. July–August 1925.

I have lived in rooms

I have lived in rooms
where I could hear myself
sniffle with the glooms,
for apparently the rooms
to which I then was fated
would contract and expand
like living creatures, and
inside of them I drowned
or had been suffocated.
                    Then again
some rooms gyrated round me
as if in fairystory rings,
galleries and towers, so
high they gave me vertigo.
Once I had a place
inside a cigarette case.
Just you think –
could a person deeper sink?
But here and now and at a table
quietly I'm sitting tight
and in the night

if I'm woken up, for once,
comes to me the pleasurable
thought: I'm one among the sons
of the working people.

M 148a. December 1925.

Börne said Heine had no character

Börne said Heine had no character;
the latter laughed at character of any kind.
A lack of character is naturally pliant,
because having character presupposes firmness.
It's what you are born to, one or the other,
brings either into life. Grillparzer,
a character to the hilt, wasn't he vexed
almost every day he lived? Even the last
Carbonari shown to us by Stendhal in one
of his novellas, did he not, heroically
enduring, resemble utterly sensitive Büchner,
who, just in time, before his littleness
was caught, escaped and fled to Zürich,
whence he wrote touching letters to the girl
he left behind? These days
there is much talk about a European
triumphing at the current Book Fair, but
who displayed, while still alive,
a medley of strength and frailty and of shoes
he had himself to mend with cotton thread.
Compassion and, for human beings, love
are what his genius consisted of.

M 099. February–March 1927.

"Apparently you're very poor"

"Apparently you're very poor,"
announced a rich industrial magnate,
and with a mocking smile he scanned the plate
from which the hero of the quill, although
the boor called him a parasite,
drew some delight.
The starveling, a reflective type
who fought,
accordingly for liberty of thought,
boldly controlled, first, his displeasure, then
with warm and cordial voice could pipe
his well-prepared reply, faster, quite a bit,
than the industrial master
anticipated: "Sir, you are full of shit!"
and lo, the high-
stepper who was short on social graces,
some years afterward, because his
business had gone bust, so that he stood
inglorious on the brink of beggarhood,
one fine day died
of suicide.

M 051. May–June 1927.

Little flowers stand in the field

Little flowers stand in the field,
little birdies flit and sing;
all along the coppice edge
I catch the whiffs of Spring.

Assuming I make no mistake,
flower petals are like lips.
A while ago I saw myself
drinking coffee, little sips.

Life, how lovely now it is!
Old acquaintances come by,
relatives also gather round
or strain themselves to fly.

Flowers and little birdies seem,
now it occurs to me,
to be believing they are one,
like song to sing and eyes to see.

Quietly, what's gone for good
comes back again aflutter.
I heard songs of Spring just now
while I was eating jam and butter.

Go traveling, just as you please,
north and south and west.
Can flowers in a field
leave anyone depressed?

Wandering aflutter makes them
duty bound to places fixed.
Each is exactly like another
as one wave is to one that's next.

Earth is a house with passageways
and rooms where you abide,
it is the storm and stress in it
that hurry me outside.

M 029. June 1927.

You fool, you do not know the ways of children

You fool, you do not know the ways of children,
you think that when it's chilly in the winter
cheeks get redder and the merry springtime
is like a child and that, for decency,
an old man has to totter through the ice and
the autumn and the summer are the pleasures
which start in ripeness, gradually wilting
and, my, how you love the sound of children's voices,
and boys who with their snowballs in the winter
knock your top hat off, you find them kind of
cavalierish, and the sick who stagger
down the narrow alleys, they've a magic
which makes you kind of sad. As for me now,
I find, with your permission, that the Spring is
primeval as massive rock and autumn
a brown jug in a blue room, and the winter
a juvenile who's clothed in a white sheepskin,
summer an imagining of corn, mosquitos
and picnic boxes. Multitudes of un-
grownupnesses are pullulating in
the adults, and in children things abound
you wouldn't like to see. You think he must be
twelve, but he is ninety, if you crack
a joke, believing children happy creatures,

he looks at you and, captive in his features,
what weariness; the stony eyeball sees
but veils an intrepidity, the enigma there
makes you go weak at the knees. Brave
enough, the thought there's a child to save
or guide, you'll sink it quickly rather
into the self such thoughts of yours conceal.
Shame is what children often make me feel.

M 425. September 1927.

Indescribably rich my attire

Indescribably rich my attire
I lay in a chamber of glass,
in a bed the pillows of which,
like radiant light from many candles,
were dazzlingly reflected, as if
themselves they felt to be enchanted,
and in comfort most refined I was
reading books, of which the content
made me the happiest inhabitant of
the star they call this earth. Imploring
at the glass wall my comrade stood.
That he was deep in trouble I could see
from his wasted face, the winter
pierced his flimsy suit
which made him look a clown. Although
I knew that nature had given him
a pleasant character, of a value which
prevented him with getting on in life,
although I saw him out there like a beggar
fastening his enormous timid Christmas
eyes like shattered glasses on
the radiance that shimmered all around me,
I did as if his misery did not exist,
went on reading, while in every street

now the Jesus bells were ringing.
Comradeship makes one uneasy, love
stands in books where stories also
stand, written, where, having given
gifts to the tiny children, up to heaven
the angel flies again.
O, the tears he wept!

M 406. October 1927.

The town might well be built of porcelain

The town might well be built of porcelain,
the streets are shimmering like mosaic
and how fresheningly unprosaic
the cuddle is for baby in a mother's lap,
entrancing too how wide
the baby eyes are open, just you look,
so open-wide the tiny thing can't smile.
Its tiny nose, gracefully curved, meanwhile,
looks just as if it flitted to the face
which looks around, aware of nothing at all.
Isn't the little child
like a breeze blowing wild,
does it understand the man one sees,
what can he want, flexing his knees,
nothing but a snuggle
and prone unconsciousness —
that it cannot understand
what's up in all the land
is a future in its glory.
The mother watches o'er the
baby very sweetly, not amazed,
nor are other people that one sees,
they have not yet

perceived the light's origination,
but go about as usual
giving all
their strength, no less,
to their daily business.
No marvel ever caused such marvellings
that they could stop the normal run of things.

M 412b. November–December 1927.

Only half an hour ago

Only half an hour ago
someone softly blew a flute;
I was sitting with my woe
in a cheery tavern room
like a callow yokel lad
whose looks improve when he is sad.

Now in a world that's wide and big,
where winds without a language blow,
with heaven above and earth below
suddenly I saw me standing;
through the pallor and the pink
wandering the flute notes flow.

Yellower the prospect grew:
"Russian student girl," said I
to myself, and heaved a sigh,
"where O where will I have found thee?"
Still as quietly the flute
drew a sort of circle round me.

M 407a (illustrated opposite). November–December 1927.

There still is something fine, for sure, about us

There still is something fine, for sure, about us,
but then the beggar boy intruded on our circle,
since then our ranks are scattered and we go,
each, in his own direction, each of us pursues
his path, and on those paths, on all
we see his face and take delight in it.
If only we had never done so. Still there is
something fine about us, something reliable. We,
even today, think we are kind and good
and never do we doubt our own opinion.
Besides, we were, regrettably, it seems,
too vitally involved with him. Why was he
the target of our merriment so often?
Don't people prone to laughter finally
make themselves laughable? Could we but free
ourselves from him, the boy whose luckless face
amused us for too long, perhaps. Once,
to see that he was beautiful made us likewise,
to take him seriously made us more serious,
to value him more highly than we do today
made us more valuable. Could we just
forget him, boy no longer one of us

but whom we see, all the same, wherever
paths no longer paths of ours may take us?
The beggar boy perhaps is like the wind,
life, forever trickling away.

M 446. December 1927–May 1928.

Ways there are that in themselves aren't new

Ways there are that in themselves aren't new
but just because nobody for the longest time
has trodden them, then they do seem new,
and what is new is always advantageous,
making you young again. Forgotten ways,
when you have, for once, found them again,
seem younger than the ones they were before.
The seeming in itself is something beautiful.
There was a sort of shimmer on the way
I walked on yesterday for the first time in years.
It is knowledge that imposes age on things,
and everything I love, by questioning it daily,
I do take value from. Things forgotten
stay forever young and beautiful.
Anyone whom you forget can be
glad of it, since thinking of those you love
takes everything away, and so they disappear.
Things thought bore through life a hole
as running water bores one in a rock.
Ways there are, people too, who stay
just as they are because you have forgotten them.
Whoever thinks of you, thinks on you to sup;
once forgotten, you won't be gobbled up.

M 073a. 1928.

This life, how old it is

This life, how old it is. Even the golden
forests and the red lips of people.
Time was when people thought that they were young,
but others came before them, younger still,
who grew like plants. Every flower
is young because it does not think, but is,
and is nobler than the lovely noble minds
of people who just know, alas, their loveliness:
the loveliness of a dog is of a better kind,
shapelier than the kind a human shows.
Does death disgust us for the reason
that we in fact are much too fond of life?
When a plant dies, does it think of something?
Does a violet have a feeling when it fades?
By the loveliness of a fish how touched we are,
no legs, no hands, the round enormous eyes!

M 059a. Spring 1928.

The houses do not blow but stand robust

The houses do not blow but stand robust,
and fugitive things, gipsyings, jokes,
do not have claws, and flowers, in my
opinion, cannot burst. Do they collapse,
the years? No. Are the trees rigid as walls?
Once there was a schoolmarm, ah, but wait,
first there was a bungler, who, with bunglings,
was quite an excellent poet, and the schoolmarm,
she loved a youngster bumpkin off the farm.
Both hearts, should she have supplicated them?
Astonishing, what wishes lurk within.
The schoolmarm I was speaking of had lots
of talent, zest for music and the waltz.
Now I adduce a woman who was rich,
to whom a deucèd pauper chose to stretch
his hands out, but her countenance remained
motionlessly obdurate and beautiful,
and, come the Spring, it's welcomer to tell
nothing about it, but to feel springily and watch
winds gusting away across the houses, now
suddenly standing, fifty, in a copse.

M 056b. April 1928.

Yes, I confess that for some years past

Yes, I confess that for some years past
I lacked the zest needed just to live,
except that on my ramblings in the backstreets
I never let myself collapse, but rather
from fields of feeling that were colorless
I swung myself up into the rosy ones, of course
that sounds a bit romantic. Truth to tell,
I became bloated with my zest, knowingly,
and trotted along to find in it myself
when really it was not there, and only
self-enchantment made me young. I never ceased
instructing life to be a help to me,
and all the time it was my projection,
as in a mirror, of any amount of things,
and if there's valor in behaving so
I simply do not know, for all that I tried
not to go down too soon into dejection.

M 204. Autumn 1928. Original rhymed throughout.

Not that I intend this to have a political sense

Not that I intend this to have a political sense,
no, not at all, biography of another, tenderer sort
is what I will sketch here, say that she has
an unutterably significant behind.
With a deep cleavage she looked enchantingly fine
and would sit with propriety never before beheld,
a tuft of feathers tucked in her hair,
gleaming and gracious there at a table-d'hôte.
If she passes me by, she measures me not
with a single glance, not even the tiniest. Years
she lived in solitude, whisking down alleyways,
claiming, fabulously, that she was an Empress. Once
she gave me a smile, and I feel it was
a thousand years since ever she did so, not
that the lady was elegant, that I demur to claim,
yet with her eyebrows alone,
which seemed to belong to a countess,
she possibly could in my maybe a bit
arch-professorial view resolve
all the problems besetting our continent. Her hand,
O how beautiful! Only to kiss it was all

the sum, for months, of my wishes; index enough
of her merit, the worth she presented, enchantress.
I alone in reality know her,
the lady who calls herself Empress Europa.

M 116a. December 1928.

PREVIOUS TRANSLATIONS INTO ENGLISH

By Susan Bernofsky:

Masquerade and Other Stories. Baltimore: Johns Hopkins
    University Press, 1990.

The Robber (novel). Lincoln: University of Nebraska Press,
    2000.

The Assistant (novel). New York: New Directions, 2007.

The Tanners (novel). New York: New Directions, 2009.

Microscripts. New York: New Directions and Christine Burgin.

By Christopher Middleton:

The Walk and Other Stories. London: John Calder, 1957.

Jakob von Gunten (novel), Austin: University of Texas Press,
    1969. (New York: Vintage Books, 1983; New York: New
    York Review Books, 1999.)

Selected Stories. New York: Farrar, Straus, and Giroux, 1983.
    (New York: New York Review Books, 2002.)

"A Painter's Life," in *Robert Walser and the Visual Arts,*
    edited by Tamara Evans. New York: CUNY Graduate
    Studies, 1996.

Speaking to the Rose: Writings 1912–32. Lincoln: University
    of Nebraska Press, 2005. (Includes the first translations
    into English of prose microscripts; translations of
    microscript poems appeared in *PN Review* 140 [2001].)

By Tom Whalen:

Several stories in *Selected Stories* (see above).

Walser Wandering. Black River Falls, WI: Obscure
    Publications, 2009 (pamphlet with three texts).

By Mark Harman:

Ten stories and three poems in *Robert Walser Rediscovered*,
    edited by Mark Harman. Hanover, NH: University
    Press of New England, 1985 (includes Walter Arndt's
    translations of two dramolets [little verse plays, 1900–
    20], "Cinderella" and "Snow White").

"The Child," in *Comparative Criticism*, Cambridge:
    Cambridge University Press, 1984.

"Green," in *Georgia Review* 45, 2 (1991).

"Well Then," in *Review of Contemporary Fiction* 12, 3 (1992).